# Y IS FOR YET

## A GROWTH MINDSET ALPHABET

by Shannon Anderson

illustrated by Jacob Souva

free spirit
PUBLISHING®

**Library of Congress Cataloging-in-Publication Data**
Names: Anderson, Shannon, 1972- author. | Souva, Jacob, illustrator.
Title: Y is for yet : a growth mindset alphabet / by Shannon Anderson ; illustrated by Jacob Souva.
Description: Minneapolis, MN : Free Spirit Publishing, [2020] | Audience: Ages 4–8
Identifiers: LCCN 2020008143 (print) | LCCN 2020008144 (ebook) | ISBN 9781631985256 (hardcover) | ISBN 9781631985263 (pdf) | ISBN 9781631985270 (epub)
Subjects: LCSH: Achievement motivation in children—Juvenile literature. | Attitude (Psychology)—Juvenile literature. | Learning, Psychology of—Juvenile literature.
Classification: LCC BF723.M56 A64 2020  (print) | LCC BF723.M56  (ebook) | DDC 153.8—dc23
LC record available at https://lccn.loc.gov/2020008143
LC ebook record available at https://lccn.loc.gov/2020008144

Edited by Alison Behnke
Cover and interior design by Shannon Pourciau

Printed in China

**Free Spirit Publishing**
An imprint of Teacher Created Materials
9850 51st Avenue North, Suite 100
Minneapolis, MN 55442
(612) 338-2068
help4kids@freespirit.com
freespirit.com

FSC
www.fsc.org
MIX
Paper | Supporting
responsible forestry
FSC® C144853

This book is dedicated to my Aunt Linda, who taught me to believe in myself and not to settle for average.

What can you do with a growth mindset?

You can strengthen your brain. You can stay positive.
You can learn from your mistakes. And so much more!

In other words . . . there's almost nothing
you *can't* do with a growth mindset!

# Aa

You have the ABILITY to do great things—especially when you have a growth mindset.

Your **BRAIN** is like a muscle. It gets stronger and stronger as you learn more and more.

You can take on CHALLENGES as opportunities to grow. Trying to do tough tasks helps your brain learn and remember.

When you are **DETERMINED**, you are committed
to accomplishing something, even if it's difficult.

# Ee

**EFFORT** and practice help you learn and grow.
We get better when we are trying our best.

**FEEDBACK** from other people gives you valuable information about how you can learn and improve even more.

**Gg**

When you make a mistake, you can think of it as a **GROWTH SPURT** that helps you learn. You learn something helpful from *every* setback you face.

Asking for **HELP** when you need it is a strong and positive choice to make.

## Ii

You can use the power of **IMAGINATION** to help develop your growth mindset. What might you do with all that you learn?

Learning something new takes you on a **JOURNEY** that may have many ups and downs. It is rare to master a task or a skill the first time you try it.

# Kk

You gain **KNOWLEDGE** by practicing until you get better. What would you like to know or practice?

There's almost no limit to the knowledge and skills you can **LEARN**! Your brain has the ability to keep learning for your whole life.

$H_2O$

CARING FOR PLANTS

PLANT LIFE

SOIL

# Mm

A **MINDSET** is your attitude or your set of beliefs. Having a growth mindset helps you stay positive and believe in yourself.

When you're striving for your goals, **NOTICE** what works well—and not so well. Both will give you useful information.

## Oo

**OPTIMISM** is trying to see some good in every situation. When you can see the positive, you can also see opportunities.

**PROGRESS**—not perfection—is a goal you can achieve each day. You can think of it like this: "In some small way, I get better every day!"

You learn by asking QUESTIONS and seeking answers.
What are you curious about?

Qq

SUPER PLANTS

GROWING!

WORLD'S LARGEST TREE

THE RAINFOREST

FORESTRY

You are **RESILIENT** when you bounce back from setbacks or obstacles. Struggle can help you grow stronger.

**Ss**

SETTING GOALS is the first step toward accomplishing them. A positive goal helps you focus, plan, and succeed.

**TRYING** hard means using different strategies, seeking advice or support, and persevering until you succeed.

You may have to keep working hard at something UNTIL you figure it out.
Try not to give up! Your work will be worth it.

**V**ISUALIZE what it will be like when you meet your goals. How do you think you'll feel when you see the results of your effort?

Ww

You can't always get what you wish for,
but you often *can* get what you **WORK** for.
What do you want to work toward?

Sometimes it takes EXTRA time and effort to accomplish something—especially something difficult or important. But if you stick with it, your determination will pay off!

# Yy

If you feel there is something you cannot do, remember the word YET. "I can't solve this problem *yet*, but if I keep trying I know I can get there."

**ZANY** ideas can lead to amazing possibilities.

With a growth mindset, you can make remarkable discoveries.

Now you know how powerful your brain can be when you have a positive approach to learning and doing new things.

¿CÓMO ESTÁS?

ROCK STAR

How will you use your growth mindset?

Ready, set . . . GROW!

# Glossary

**ability:** the power or skill to do something

**accomplish:** to do or to finish a task

**attitude:** the way you think or feel about someone or something

**determined:** having a strong feeling or being very decided about something

**feedback:** information that one person gives another to help them improve

**opportunity:** the chance to do something

**persevere:** to keep trying or working toward an achievement, even when it gets hard

**positive:** having a good attitude and looking on the bright side

**resilient:** able to bounce back and try again after facing a challenge

**setback:** a difficulty or obstacle that causes your progress to slow or stop

**strategies:** ways you try to achieve a goal or solve a problem

**strive:** to work hard toward a goal

**visualize:** to create a picture in your mind

# Helping Kids Embrace the Power of Yet: Activities to Build a Growth Mindset

You can use the activities in this section to explore, build, and strengthen a growth mindset in the kids you work with—whether you're a teacher, counselor, family member, or other caring adult. Feel free to adapt these in ways that work best for your group. (Most of these activities also work well if you're reading the book one-on-one!)

## MINDSET MATCH-UP

Talk with kids about the difference between having a growth mindset versus a fixed mindset. A growth mindset is the belief that you can learn or improve at anything with enough practice and time. Someone with a growth mindset understands that they learn from mistakes and that challenges help them grow. A fixed mindset is the belief that there's a limit to ability or intelligence. Someone with a fixed mindset may give up when a new skill becomes hard, thinking they can't do it and might as well not try to get better.

To explore these ideas further, play a match-up game. You'll need fixed-mindset statements paired with growth-mindset statements on notecards. Write one statement on each notecard and make sure each is paired with another statement demonstrating the opposite mindset. Ideally, you will have one card for each student. (If you have an odd number of kids in your group, you could have one of the cards yourself.) For example:

| Fixed-Mindset Statements | Growth-Mindset Statements |
| --- | --- |
| ✳ I'm not good at math. | ✳ I'm learning more math facts every day. |
| ✳ I can't draw. | ✳ My drawings aren't great yet, but they're getting better. |
| ✳ I'm no good at making friends. | ✳ I'm a good friend and I can work on meeting new people. |
| ✳ I'm bad at sports. | ✳ I can keep practicing my sports skills. |
| ✳ My handwriting is terrible. | ✳ I can improve my handwriting with practice. |

Pass out the notecards and have kids move around the space, talking and comparing thoughts to match up the pairs of growth-mindset and fixed-mindset cards. When they feel they have matched all the cards, have students read them aloud. Discuss who has the growth-mindset cards and who has the fixed-mindset cards and which ones they relate to most. Did anyone disagree on what statements showed which mindset?

## MY BUMPY BRAIN

Kids love learning about their brains! In this activity, explain how our brains have billions of tiny nerve cells called neurons. Our neurons send messages to each other as we learn and practice skills.

Have each kid draw a bumpy oval representing their brain. Next, have them draw eight to ten neurons inside the brain. (They can just draw dots for these, or they can get more creative if they choose!) Ask kids to think of a skill they have practiced a lot and are good at. Suppose it is tying their shoes. Kids can draw a thick line connecting two dots (neurons) and write "tying my shoes" on the line.

Now have kids think of something they have not learned to do well yet. Maybe it is learning to multiply. Have them draw a thin or dotted line connecting two different dots and write "multiply numbers" on the dotted line.

Discuss how their drawings represent how we learn. As we practice and learn something, the pathways connecting our neurons get stronger. We can picture this as a line that gets thicker and thicker the more we practice and learn a new skill. The thicker the line, the more easily we can do the skill. For example, once you've mastered riding a bike, you don't have to think about it so hard to do it successfully. But if we stop practicing a skill for a long time, the pathways may start to weaken. That is why it is so important to keep practicing and reviewing skills.

## PUTTING OUR NEURONS TO THE TEST

Think of something you can teach your group that would be interesting to kids and that not many of them know how to do *yet*. Perhaps it is writing the Roman numerals from one to twenty, counting in another language up to twenty, signing the alphabet in American Sign Language, or memorizing a poem. (You could come up with a list of four or five options and have kids vote on which goal you will conquer as a class.)

Once you've picked a goal, spend three weeks practicing the skill as a group for five to ten minutes each day. Have each kid keep a daily progress log as you practice, giving themselves a rating on a scale of one to ten according to how well they feel they're doing the task or skill. Maybe on the first day, they give themselves a rating of one or two. At the end of the three weeks, they will ideally be rating themselves at a nine or ten. By doing this activity, they see that progress takes time and practice. Talk about how it felt to learn and strengthen the skill. Was it ever frustrating? Exciting? Discouraging? Positive? How did they handle these feelings?

*Variation:* You could combine this activity with "My Bumpy Brain" and have kids draw a dotted line between two neurons on their brain pictures at the start of the three weeks of learning, making the line heavier and thicker as they strengthen their neural pathways supporting this new skill.

## PREPARING FOR GROWTH SPURTS

A growth spurt is when you have a setback as you are learning something new. It can be frustrating when you try really hard and still make mistakes or fail. The good news is that we learn and grow from our mistakes and trials. You can help kids prepare for these trials ahead of time by having them create motivational messages to post in your space. Ask students to create small posters featuring positive statements to help them remember to keep trying and not give up. Examples might be:

* "I can do this!"
* "I've got what it takes!"

* "In some small way, I get better every day."
* "It's going to feel so good when I reach my goal."
* "Keep moving forward."
* "My hard work will be worth it."
* "Stay strong and don't give up."
* "I can learn from my mistakes."

When you see a student struggling, remind them to look at the motivation wall and read some words of encouragement. Remind them that growth spurts are part of the process, and that we can grow and get better with more practice and time.

## TO-DO AND TO-DON'T LISTS

Kids have probably heard of to-do lists, but may not have ever made a to-don't list. Ask kids to think of the things they would write on a to-do list if they wanted to make more friends. You might write things like:

* Be kind to others.
* Ask someone to play during recess.
* Give someone a compliment.
* Help someone with a task.
* Smile often.

If you made a to-don't list for making friends, it might look like this:

* Tease others.
* Ignore kids who talk to you.
* Laugh when someone trips or spills.
* Roll your eyes when someone talks.
* Frown at people.

As you discuss an example like this, it might seem funny or silly to kids, but at the same time it will build their understanding of what kinds of actions may help them reach a goal, and what may prevent them from attaining a goal. Have kids write a goal at the top of a sheet of paper. Then have them write two or three to-do steps and two or three to-don't steps. If kids are willing to share, you could invite some to read their lists and talk about how they made them.

## TWENTY QUESTIONS

This simple game is one kids may have played before, and it is a good way to illustrate how we can learn from our mistakes. Have a student come to the front of the room and face the group. Write a number on the board above their head, and don't allow them to see what it is. Then have the student ask the rest of the group questions to try to figure out what the number is.

Through the student's questions—*and* through their incorrect guesses—they will get closer and closer to the right number. If the student guesses the right number before they have asked twenty questions, they win.

Low-risk games like this help kids see how we learn from feedback as well as from our growth spurts. If they think back to learning to ride a bike or watching a younger sibling or cousin learn to walk, they know that learning happens through trial and error. When playing a game like twenty questions, no one would expect someone to guess the correct number on the first try—just as no one would expect someone to take off riding a bike the first time they get on one.

## CELEBRATE SUCCESS!

Create a spot in the room where kids can celebrate their progress, milestones, and accomplishments. Stock the celebration area with fun items like small instruments, clappers, buttons that make celebratory noises when pressed, sections of bubble wrap to pop, nerf rocket launchers, or fun stickers. These items could be displayed on a table or in a special box. When students reach a goal, they can spend a minute or two in this area using one of the items.

Kids work hard on their goals and deserve to celebrate a job well done. The act of getting up and celebrating an accomplishment for a moment feels good and can motivate others to keep going too.

# About the Author and Illustrator

**Shannon Anderson** is an award-winning children's book author and loves to do author visits to teach the power of reading, writing, and learning with a growth mindset. She has taught for 25 years, from first grade through college level. Shannon also held the roles of gifted coordinator, literacy coach, and adjunct professor. A highlight of her teaching career was being named one of ten teachers who "amazed and inspired us" by the Today Show. You can learn more about her at shannonisteaching.com. She lives in Indiana.

**Jacob Souva, BFA,** loves to make kids laugh and think with his illustration work. He sketches constantly and finishes his work digitally, placing a lot of emphasis on simple shapes, color, and lots and lots of texture. He has a beautiful wife and two amazing sons, and resides in a small countryside community in upstate New York.